CONTENTS

WHY ARE BUGS SO GREAT?

Bugs are essential to life on Earth. Without bugs, plants would not be able to make flowers or fruit. If bugs disappeared, so would strawberries, apples, oranges, pears, beans, chocolate, tomatoes and much more.

Bugs help not only plants to make food, but also farmers and gardeners, too. Bugs make the soil rich and healthy. Without them, we couldn't grow enough food to feed us all.

As well as helping to make food, bugs are food themselves! They are eaten by wild animals and birds. If we lost bugs, we would also lose many creatures, such as songbirds, bats, frogs and freshwater fish. Our countryside would be empty and silent.

First published in 2022 by Wayland
Copyright in the text © Hodder and Stoughton 2022
Copyright in the illustrations © QU Lan 2022

Wayland, an imprint of Hachette Children's Group
Part of Hodder and Stoughton
Carmelite House
50 Victoria Embankment
London EC4Y 0DZ

Editor: Victoria Brooker
Inside design: Lisa Peacock
Cover design: Claire Jones

HB ISBN: 9781526313850
PB ISBN: 9781526313867

MIX
Paper from
responsible sources
FSC® C104740

Printed in China

Wayland is a division of
Hachette Children's Books,
an Hachette UK company.
www.hachette.co.uk

All creatures have a special place in the web of life. Each does a particular job that helps another creature, including humans. Each job is important and, once lost, creatures cannot be replaced. Just like a spider's delicate and beautiful web, the web of life works properly only if every tiny section of it holds firm. Bugs need your help and understanding.

We're going to look at bugs' place in the web of life. You can also find out what you can do to protect bugs.

CAN BUGS REALLY SAVE THE WORLD?

WHAT ARE BUGS?

Bugs belong to a group of animals called invertebrates. These animals do not have a backbone. They make up around two thirds of all living things on our planet.

VERTEBRATES

Vertebrates are animals that do have a backbone. They are split into five groups: mammals, birds, amphibians, reptiles and fish. Many of our planet's vertebrates rely on bugs to survive (they eat them).

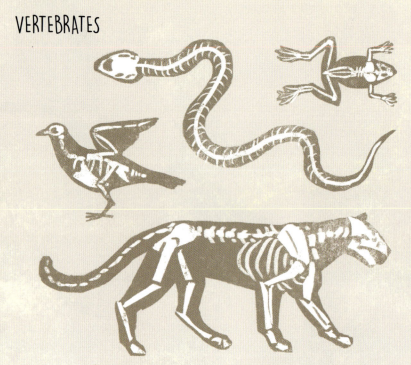

INVERTEBRATES

Invertebrates come in all shapes, sizes and colours. They can be found living on land, in the sea, in lakes and rivers, in the ground and even in the air. Invertebrates are often called bugs, although some people only think of insects as bugs. They are the real-life superheroes of planet Earth.

THESE ARE JUST A FEW OF THE IMPORTANT JOBS THAT BUGS DO:

- POLLINATION (SEE PAGES 10–15, 20)

- SPREADING SEEDS (SEE PAGE 17)

- IMPROVING SOIL (SEE PAGE 22)

- PEST CONTROL (SEE PAGES 21, 24–25)

- BREAKING DOWN/RECYCLING (SEE PAGES 26–29)

- PROVIDING FOOD (SEE PAGE 34)

- HELPING IN MEDICINE (SEE PAGES 36–37)

- MAKING MONEY (SEE PAGE 38).

LET'S LOOK
IN MORE DETAIL
AT THESE SUPERHERO TASKS.

SUPER WORMS

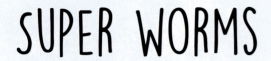

Feeding the world's enormous population is no small task. Luckily some long, wriggly invertebrate superheroes can help!

Earthworms spend their time burrowing in the ground under our feet. They eat dead leaves and plants and then wriggle through the soil. Their droppings add rich nutrients to the soil. Their burrowing tunnels make paths for air and water to travel underground. When they die, earthworm bodies decompose and add even more nutrients to the soil.

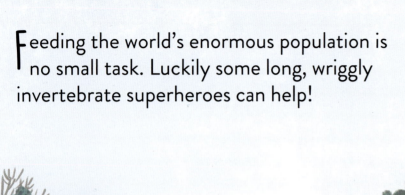

Earthworm tunnels loosen the soil so that the roots of trees and plants can grow more easily. Worms are also delicious food for creatures, such as foxes, birds and toads.

Although earthworms are helpful to farmers, they are in trouble! Many farming methods damage worms and their habitat. Ploughing, using chemicals, or just over-using the land so that it becomes dry and hard kills worms. Changing farming methods and looking after the soil will help earthworms to thrive and be able to keep making healthy soil. This will boost food crops and help farmers.

POWERFUL POLLINATORS

Did you know that an apple produced from a tree with good pollination will have more seeds and will grow bigger and juicer to protect the seeds? If you were buying apples, what would you choose – a small apple or a big juicy one?

Pollination is the movement of pollen from one flower to another. Passing pollen on allows flowers to make seeds. Plants make seeds so that more plants can grow. Pollen can be carried by the wind, animals or water, but mainly it is moved by insects.

Much of the food we eat depends on the plant being pollinated. Plants, such as cucumbers, tomatoes, beans and peas, must all be pollinated before they can produce these fruit. Other plants, such as carrots, need pollination to make seeds.

Most people know that bees pollinate, but did you know that wasps, butterflies, beetles and even flies do, too? Globally there are more than 100,000 different bugs that help with pollination!

Most wildflowers and many garden flowers need pollination. Even trees, that look so tall and strong, need tiny creatures to help with pollination. If pollinators disappear, trees and plants will, too.

LET'S FIND OUT MORE ABOUT SUPERHERO POLLINATORS!

BRILLIANT BEES

When we think about bees, we often imagine them making honey, but only a few bee types produce honey. Honeybees lives in a hive and make honey to feed the colony over winter when food is scarce. They make more than they need so many people keep beehives and harvest the extra honey for food.

Honeybees are pollinators and they visit lots of different food sources. Other wild bees have their favourite flowers. This makes them better pollinators as they move between plants of the same kind ensuring good pollen transfer.

There are around 20,000 bee species worldwide – just nine of these are honeybees and 250 of these are bumblebees. Many bee species are known as solitary bees. Solitary bees are thought to be 300 times better at pollination than honeybees.

Bees rely on flowers for pollen and nectar. In cooler regions, they often hibernate through the colder months. But as the planet warms up, they are increasingly in need of year-round food supplies. This is a problem as there are fewer flowers in the winter months.

In a few provinces of China, pollination is now being undertaken by hand using paintbrushes because there are fewer bees left to do it naturally. Bees are declining all over the world due to our use of pesticides and the loss of their natural habitats. Large fields and open spaces have been replaced by buildings or fields for farming that lack the variety and amount of flowers that are needed to support bees.

BEAUTIFUL BUTTERFLIES & MOTHS

Scientists study butterflies and moths because they can tell us a lot about the state of wildlife today. Butterflies and moths are probably the best recorded bug type, so changes in their numbers and behaviour can be tracked easily. The changes that are happening to them are usually happening to other bugs, too.

Butterflies and moths are pollinators. Their long tongues, called proboscis, can reach down flowers that other pollinators might not be able to reach. They travel for long distances looking for particular nectar-rich flowers, which they find through smell. Growing butterfly- and moth-friendly plants in your garden can help them to refuel when travelling.

As well as being useful pollinators, butterflies and moths lay eggs that hatch into caterpillars. These are an important food for other wildlife.

Many moths are night-time fliers and they are attracted to light. This means that when they should be pollinating flowers, many fly into streetlamps, garden or house lights. Unfortunately, one in three doesn't survive the experience of flying too close to a light. Every night, we are killing these precious creatures.

Help marvellous moths by shutting the curtains at night.
Ask your parents to turn off any outside lights overnight.

MIMIC HOVERFLIES

Hoverflies are copycats! They mimic the look of wasps and bees to protect themselves from predators. They do lots of good jobs for the planet, including pollinating, pest control and cleaning.

Adult hoverflies eat pollen and nectar so they are great pollinators. They often migrate long distances –even across continents!

The larvae of some hoverfly species eat plant pests, such as lice and aphids, whilst others eat dead or decaying plants.

The larva of the hornet hoverfly can live happily in wasp nests without getting stung! They eat the debris and rubbish in the nest, keeping it clean for the wasps and their larvae.

FARMER ANTS

Black ants build their nests in soil and, like earthworms, mix it up and help it to stay healthy. Ants store seeds in their nests, which helps plants to thrive because some of these seeds will grow into new plants.

Black ants eat other insects and sugary substances, such as rotting fruit. In this way they help to control pests and tidy up the countryside.

Ants also farm aphids. Aphids are small bugs that feed on plant sap, often damaging plants. However, they are important as food for lots of other creatures. Ants protect aphids, collect the sugary honeydew that they produce, and carry them to fresh plants to feed. They also take some aphids underground over winter for food and to protect them from the cold to establish new aphid farms in the spring.

CLEVER BEETLES

The world has an extraordinary number of beetles – around 1.5 million species – and there is little they can't do!

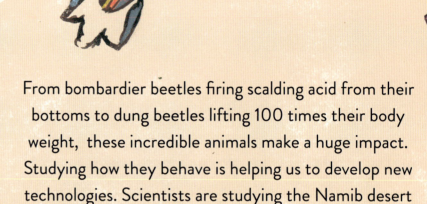

From bombardier beetles firing scalding acid from their bottoms to dung beetles lifting 100 times their body weight, these incredible animals make a huge impact. Studying how they behave is helping us to develop new technologies. Scientists are studying the Namib desert beetle to see how we can learn how to harvest water from the air, which has the potential to keep plants and people alive in harsh environments, including during space exploration.

Beetles pollinated the first flowers at the time of the dinosaurs, more than 140 million years ago. Because of this we now have an abundance of flowers and pollinators.

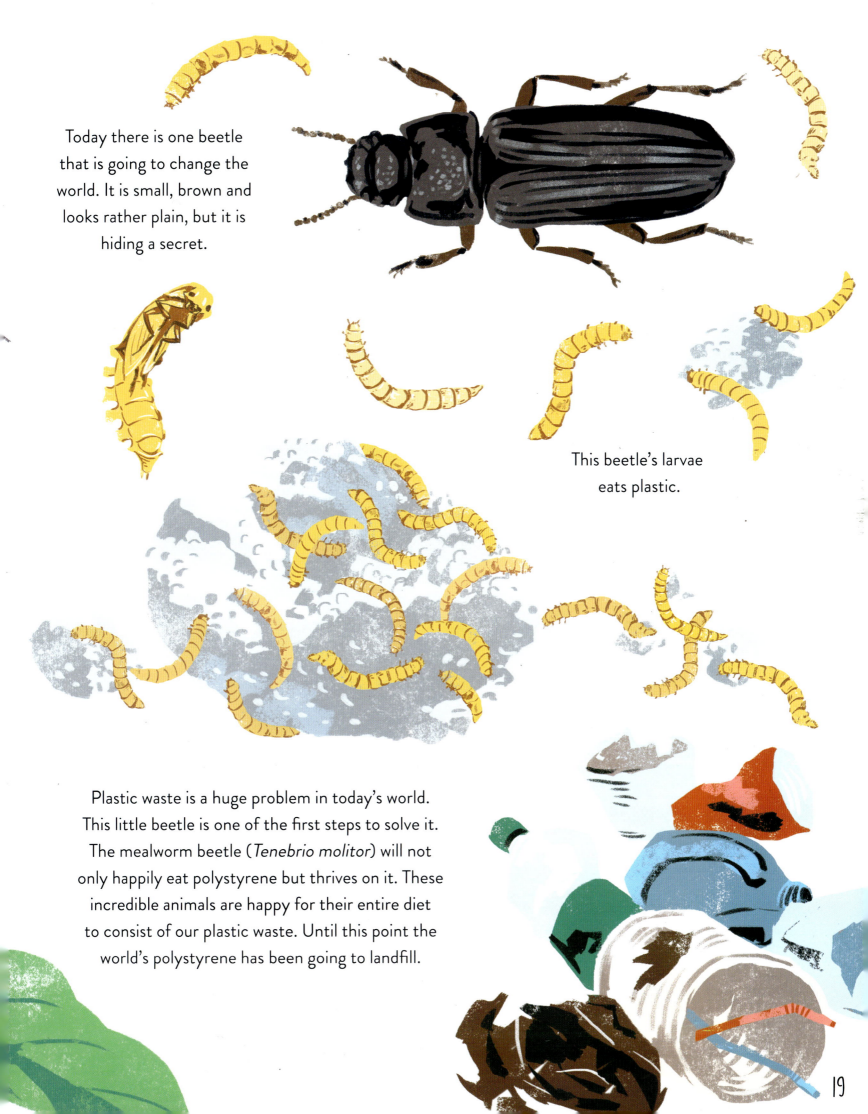

Today there is one beetle that is going to change the world. It is small, brown and looks rather plain, but it is hiding a secret.

This beetle's larvae eats plastic.

Plastic waste is a huge problem in today's world. This little beetle is one of the first steps to solve it. The mealworm beetle (*Tenebrio molitor*) will not only happily eat polystyrene but thrives on it. These incredible animals are happy for their entire diet to consist of our plastic waste. Until this point the world's polystyrene has been going to landfill.

WONDERFUL WASPS

Do you think wasps are annoying and pointless? Think again! Wasps are amazing because they do helpful jobs for our planet.

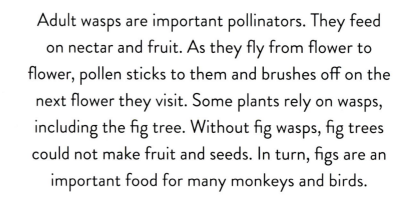

Adult wasps are important pollinators. They feed on nectar and fruit. As they fly from flower to flower, pollen sticks to them and brushes off on the next flower they visit. Some plants rely on wasps, including the fig tree. Without fig wasps, fig trees could not make fruit and seeds. In turn, figs are an important food for many monkeys and birds.

There are over 100,000 species of wasp in the world. Only around 20 species are social wasps that build large nests. These are the ones that people fear and which are likely to sting if disturbed.

Wasps are also hunters. They hunt insects and spiders to feed to their young (larvae). This helps to keep bug populations in balance in nature.

Most of the larger solitary wasps eat large numbers of caterpillars and other larvae that eat plants.

Without wasps eating these plant pests, more crops would be destroyed, or more poisonous pesticides would be used to remove these pests.

MARVELLOUS MILLIPEDES

As we have already found out, earthworms and ants help to enrich the soil. Another bug with an important job is the marvellous millipede. Millipedes are secretive animals living in soil and rotting leaves, or beneath stones, logs and bark.

They push their way through vegetation, eating and recycling dead and rotten plants. This also loosens soil and pulls nutrients down into the ground, helping plants to grow.

Millipedes are built for pushing through soil or under stones. They have lots of short legs, which can force open nooks and crannies in soil and leaf-litter. Millipedes have evolved in many different way to do this.

RAM BULLDOZERS, such as white-legged snake millipedes, tuck their head down and push forwards using lots of closely spaced, short legs. The trunk of their cylindrical body is flexible, tough and strong.

TUNNELLERS, such as pointed-head millipedes, force their head into tiny crannies. Now they use their leg muscles to pull their body forwards until the tunnel is wide enough for the rest of the body to go through.

WEDGERS, such as flat-backed millipedes, use their flat head to lift open cracks in the soil or leaf-litter and then work their flat body into crevices by opening up a wedge-shaped space.

CENTIPEDES IN ACTION!

Did you know that there might be a fearsome predator in your garden, a fast carnivore, with special legs near the front with which it can inject venom (poison) into its prey? It is, of course, the centipede!

Centipedes can be found all over the world, even in the Arctic Circle! In most places, only smaller insects need to fear this hunter. However, in the tropics there are giant centipedes capable of piercing human skin and injecting people with their venom!

When centipedes sense a possible meal nearby, they use their special legs as fangs. They inject venom into their prey so that they can overpower it. With a centipede, it can be hard to tell which end is which: the longer legs at the back look a lot like its long front antennae. It can also move backwards nearly as quickly as it scuttles forwards!

The centipede is an superhero bug because it helps us out by gobbling up garden pests. Centipedes are great at eating up slow-moving bugs such as slugs, leatherjackets and wireworms. But they are also speedy enough to hunt down fast-moving prey, including their close cousins the millipedes, woodlice and even spiders.

BODY SNATCHERS

Unpleasant thought time: when an animal, a rat or bird, for example, dies in the wild, where does its body go? Why don't we find their bodies all over the countryside? That's where bugs come in. There are two types of bug in particular who play an important role as the body snatchers.

Burying beetles, also known as sexton beetles, are brightly coloured members of a group of carrion beetles. Carrion means dead animal bodies and this is the beetles' food source. Burying beetles work in pairs to dig underneath small dead animals, burying them in a pit. Next, they create a nest and lay eggs. When the larvae hatch, they feed on the dead body recycling it into the ground.

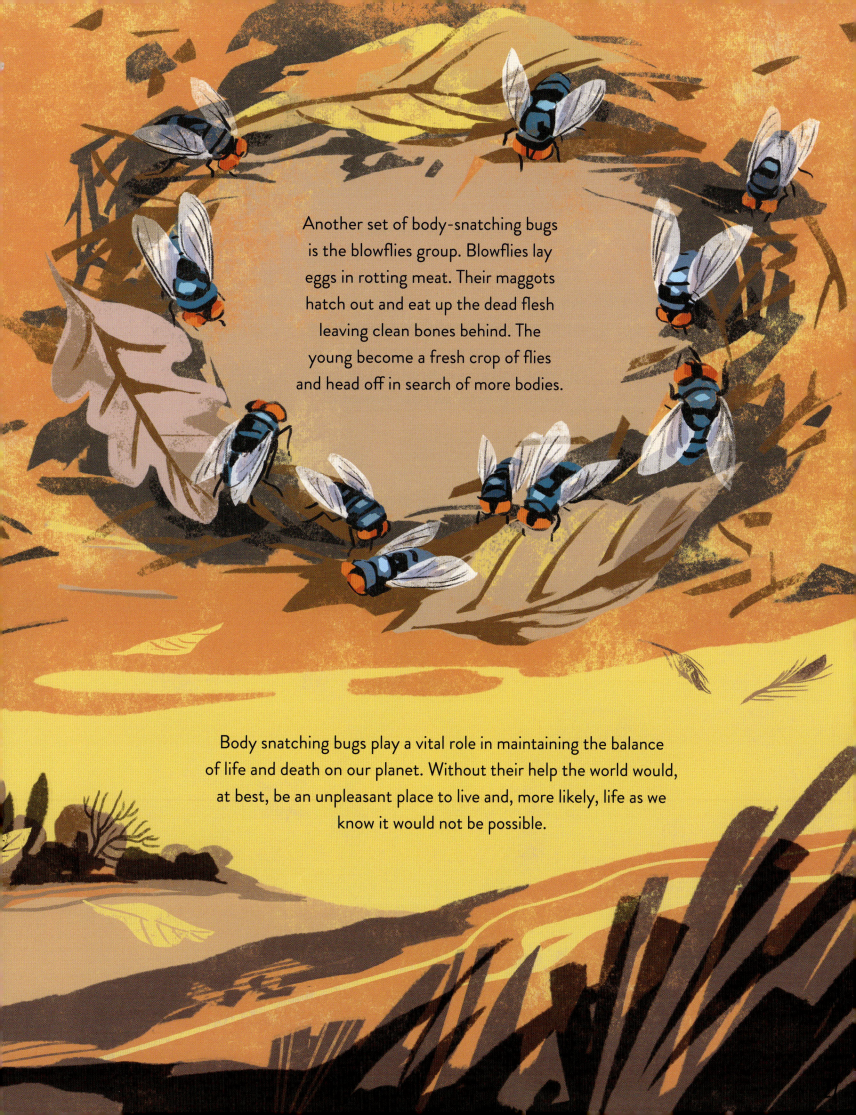

Another set of body-snatching bugs is the blowflies group. Blowflies lay eggs in rotting meat. Their maggots hatch out and eat up the dead flesh leaving clean bones behind. The young become a fresh crop of flies and head off in search of more bodies.

Body snatching bugs play a vital role in maintaining the balance of life and death on our planet. Without their help the world would, at best, be an unpleasant place to live and, more likely, life as we know it would not be possible.

POO EATERS

Spotting one dog mess when you are out for a walk isn't nice but think how bad it could be with all the animals that poo in a day, month, year, lifetime ... So, where does all the poo go?

Once more it is the bugs who come to the planet's rescue. Some of the greatest poo cleaners are dung beetles and there are three types:

1) The DWELLERS, who set up home inside the poo.

2) The TUNNELLERS, who dig under and bury the poo in the ground.

Dung beetles can bury more than 250 times their own weight in poo every day. The buried dung will become food for larvae when they hatch out of eggs laid close to the dung. Many dung beetles are fussy about their poo and will eat dung only from specific animals, whilst others are less fussy.

3) The ROLLERS, who create round balls of poo to roll away.

There are other bugs that consume poo, including many flies, but dung beetles are little heroes who do more for sanitation than our sewage systems – and help to keep our shoes clean when we are out for a walk!

WATER WONDERS

Bugs that live in our ponds, streams and rivers do an important job in keeping our water clean. They help to break down dead plants and are a food source for larger animals, such as fish, birds and mammals. Scientists use water bugs to monitor the health of water sources. Healthy water sources actually contain lots of living things.

Some insects can walk on water. Most of them are speedy – zipping in to deal with any new food source. But one, the long-legged water-measurer, likes to take its time. Water-measurers are unhurried and cautious. They are scavengers and can sense little vibrations in the surface of the water and use these to find food. They feed on the bodies of tiny animals that land on, or rise up to, the water's surface – dead or alive.

Water-measurers can also catch water fleas, mosquito larvae and other small animals moving underneath them by spearing them on needle-like mouthparts.

Many water-living bugs are now threatened because their habitat is changing. Water is becoming polluted with chemicals, stream beds and water levels are changing with human activity, and climate change is altering water temperatures. All of these things can kill off many important bugs.

SPACE TRAVELLERS

In 2007 a crew of brave bug explorers were launched into the harsh conditions of space by scientists. After ten days with no air, intense sun rays and no water, they were rehydrated and some managed to survive. A first for the animal kingdom! Meet the tardigrades.

Tardigrade means 'slow walker' and they do move very slowly. These bugs are also known as water bears because, when peered at through a microscope, they look like chubby bears with eight legs. They can be found on land, in freshwater and the sea.

Despite their tiny size, at between 0.1 and 1.2 mm, tardigrades are incredibly tough creatures. Not only can they withstand extreme pressure and temperature changes, but they can also dry out completely and come back to life again!

Tardigrades seems to go into an extreme sleep, or dormant, state. They can live for years when completely dried out and then come back to life when water becomes available again.

Learning from tardigrades may, one day, enable humans to travel deep into space or perhaps even send life on to new worlds.

BUG BANQUET

A lot of people feel sick at the thought of eating insects. However, humans eat plenty of other invertebrates – think of crabs, shellfish and scampi.

With the world's population growing, using insects as a form of food makes sense. They reproduce quite quickly, are easier to farm than birds or mammals, and do not contribute to greenhouse gases in the way that cattle do.

In some countries, insects already play an important role in providing food. It is estimated that around two billion people use insects as part of their daily diet.

In the Democratic Republic of Congo, the average household consumes 300 gm of caterpillars every week. Locusts and mealworms are just two of the bugs that can be ground down into a nutritious flour. Sugar ants are known for their sweet flavour.

If we are going to be able to continue to feed the world's vast population, while reducing climate change and protecting nature at the same time, then the farming and eating of insects is likely to become essential. Many insects can be farmed and stacked up high in industrial buildings, leaving more land free to be wild and allowing lost habitats to recover.

DOCTOR BUG

Could leeches and maggots be used by doctors? You might think the last thing that you need in a hospital is a bug, but some might be useful! Scientists study bugs' behaviour and their venoms to see how we might be able to copy them.

In the past, fly larvae (maggots) were used to treat wounds. Open wounds can quickly become infected by dead flesh. Maggots eat only dead flesh, so when they are placed on a wound, they can clean it and prevent infection. In some hospitals, maggots are once again being used to keep wounds clean.

In plastic and reconstructive surgery, leeches may be used to help blood flow. When placed on the skin, leeches bite to suck blood. When they bite, they release substances that reduce pain, prevent clotting and improve the blood supply to the area. This can re-start blood flow in small blood vessels, which prevents the new or repaired tissue from dying. Leeches were used a lot in the past, but their benefits are better understood today.

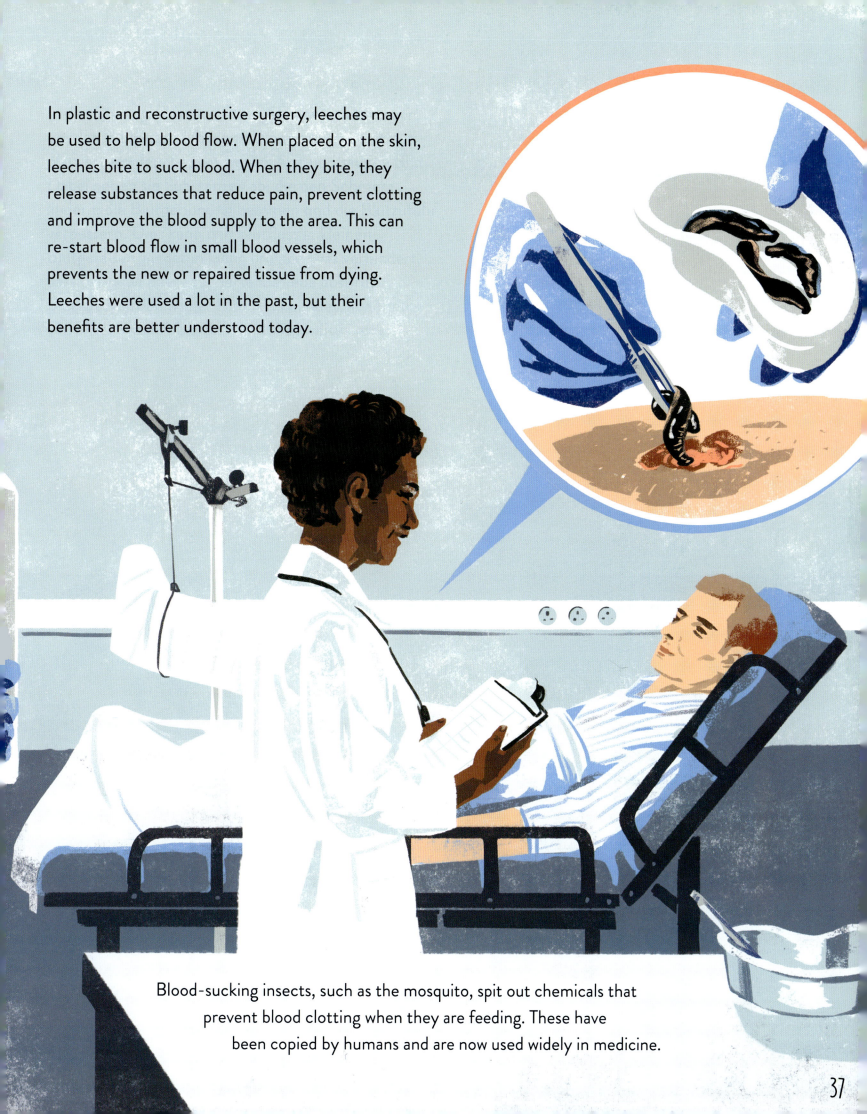

Blood-sucking insects, such as the mosquito, spit out chemicals that prevent blood clotting when they are feeding. These have been copied by humans and are now used widely in medicine.

INSECT MONEYMAKERS

Bugs are mini moneymakers! Bees take the lead in money-making with their liquid gold - honey - but other bugs are highly valued too.

Honeybees produce honey that people can sell. As well as honey, the honeybee produces wax to form cells for honey storage. This wax is extracted and used to make beeswax polish for tables, wooden floors and even leather.

Bees also make money in other ways. Farmers of almonds pay beekeepers to bring hives of bees close to their crops at key times to ensure good pollination. Greenhouse growers buy in bumblebee nests to put inside their glasshouses to provide the pollination necessary for crops such as tomatoes.

Silk comes from the cocoons of silkmoth caterpillars and has been a valuable trade for over 2,000 years. Other bugs, such as spiders, make silk, and research is underway to see if this silk can be used in new, extra-strong but lightweight fabrics.

The female lac bug secretes a resin similar to beeswax. When processed, this is called shellac and has many uses including polish for fruits, vegetables and sweets, nail varnish, fireworks and more!

WEB OF LIFE

Even if you don't want to eat insects or other bugs, they are the food source for many birds, reptiles, fish, amphibians and mammals. All of these animals are also food for other animals. If bug populations decline, it is possible our food chains would collapse.

Without bugs, the only birds to survive would be those that feed on grains and plants that do not require pollinators, and a few scavengers of carrion. This would be a handful of bird species in each country instead of a rich diversity.

Without bugs, there would be no smaller mammals, such as hedgehogs, badgers or shrews, who rely on bugs for food.

Without bugs, most of our flowers and fruiting trees would not be able to make seeds and would die out.

Without bugs, the fish in our rivers would be gone - robbed of the bugs they feast upon.

Without bugs, there would be no frogs, toads, newts and few lizards and snakes. They would have nothing to eat.

In short, if insects and other bugs were taken away, the links in the food chains would break and the web of life would collapse. The world would lose its colour, taste and sound.

THIS IS TRULY WHY BUGS ARE THE SUPERHERO SAVIOURS OF THE WORLD, FOR EVERYTHING WE TAKE FOR GRANTED IN OUR LIVES DEPENDS ON THEM.

THE FUTURE FOR BUGS

Bugs face a lot of different threats to their survival. These include:

• LOSS OF HABITAT – bugs depend on their habitat for good sources of food and somewhere to live

• LOSS OF CONNECTEDNESS – this means it is no longer possible for bugs to move from one good area of habitat to another, perhaps because of roads or buildings being built through or near their habitats

• TOXIC BUILD-UP OF CHEMICALS – chemicals used to kill pests and weeds also poison helpful bugs

• CLIMATE CHANGE – as temperatures increase, bugs need to move to a new habitat to maintain their preferred temperature

• NON-NATIVE SPECIES – bugs and plants moving between countries bring competition for already scarce food and space, and bring diseases that can destroy local populations of bugs.

These threats cannot be undone in one country alone. Worldwide, nations and organisations need to work together to stop bugs from dying out.

Governments and other authorities have an important role to play in reversing these threats.

They can:

- bring in rules to stop or change how chemicals are used,

- reward positive actions, such as considerate farming,

- support the vision for joined-up wildlife corridors across continents which will enable climate change migration and restore the connectedness of habitats,

- act to reduce greenhouse gas emissions and so reverse climate change.

Big actions are needed, but if they are planned properly then they can work. For example, a planned, joined-up network of bug-friendly habitats requires less land than if areas are chosen randomly and are not connected.

WORKING TOGETHER WITH BUGS AND WITH EACH OTHER IS THE KEY TO SUCCESS.

YOU CAN DO YOUR BIT, TOO

Our amazing hardworking superhero bugs are in trouble. Almost 40 per cent of species are threatened with extinction by 2050 if we don't change our ways.

HERE ARE SOME WAYS THAT YOU CAN HELP IN YOUR OUTSIDE SPACES.

LET YOUR GRASS GROW LONGER BETWEEN CUTS
This provides shelter for bugs and lets flowers begin to grow in the lawn. Everything needs somewhere to live, bugs included!

DON'T USE PESTICIDES AND HERBICIDES IN YOUR GARDENS
Chemicals can damage bugs' abilities to find their way around, reproduce and fight disease.

GROW POLLINATOR-FRIENDLY FLOWERS
Pollinators need a good food supply, and, with the warming climate, this food is needed all year round. You may not have a garden, but a window box or patio planter can still play an important role.

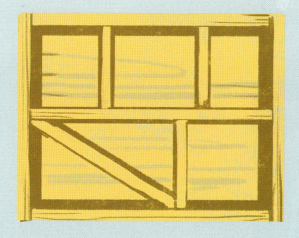

INSTALL A BUG HOME

You can make your own using an online guide or buy one from a shop.

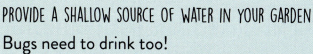

PROVIDE A SHALLOW SOURCE OF WATER IN YOUR GARDEN

Bugs need to drink too!

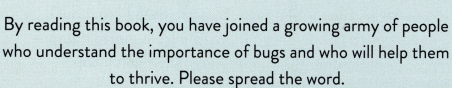

By reading this book, you have joined a growing army of people who understand the importance of bugs and who will help them to thrive. Please spread the word.

ARE YOU READY TO HELP BUGS SAVE THE WORLD?

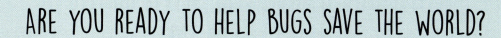

GLOSSARY

antenna One of the two long, thin parts of an insect's head, used for feel and touch.

aphid Small sap-sucking insect.

climate change A change in the normal weather around the world.

cocoon A covering of silk threads that some insects make to protect themselves when they are changing into an adult.

colony A group of animals that live together in one place, often called a nest.

decompose When dead things break down into tiny bits.

evolve To develop and change over time, often over many generations, as a result of changes in the environment.

fly A small flying insect with one pair of wings.

greenhouse gas Any one of the gases that are changing Earth's atmosphere and leading to climate change.

habitat A place or type of surroundings where living things are usually found.

hibernate A deep sleep used by some animals to survive winter.

honeydew A sweet, sticky liquid made by some insects, including aphids.

industrial Connected to industry, such as factories making goods.

insect A small animal with a body in three parts, a hard exoskeleton and six jointed legs.

larva (larvae) Insect young.

leatherjacket The larva of a crane fly.

leech A small blood-sucking worm.

lice Small insects that live on humans and animals.

maggot The young of a fly.

migrate To move from one part of the world to another, according to the seasons.

nectar A sweet liquid made by plants to attract insects to their flowers.

non-native A living thing that has been brought, or has travelled, from its usual habitat to live elsewhere.

nutrient A substance that helps plants and animals to live and grow.

pest control Reducing the number of animal (often insect) pests that are eating plants or food crops.

pesticide A chemical that is designed and used to kill pests, usually insects.

pollen A sticky, fine dust made by the male parts of a flower.

pollination This takes place when the male part (pollen) of one flower reaches the female part of another, allowing it to make fruit and seeds.

pollute To damage water, air or soil with harmful substances, such as waste, litter and man-made chemicals.

predator An animal that hunts and eats other animals.

prey An animal that is hunted and killed by another for food.

recycling Releasing and/or reusing materials locked up inside dead material or waste material.

seed A small part made by a plant, from which a new plant can grow.

species A kind of living thing, such as a hornet hoverfly, that can reproduce with others of its species.

web of life All the living things connected together in multiple food chains make up the web of life.

wildlife corridor A narrow piece of land connecting wild areas together when they have been separated by human activity, such as roads and buildings.

wireworm The young of a click beetle.

FURTHER INFORMATION

BOOKS

Endangered Wildlife: Insects and Invertebrates by Anita Ganeri (Wayland, 2018)
Meet the Minibeasts by Sarah Ridley (Wayland, 2019)
Nature Detective: British Insects by Victoria Munson (Wayland, 2016)
The Insects that Run our World series by Sarah Ridley (Wayland, 2020)

WEBSITES

BUGLIFE

www.buglife.org.uk/bugs/bug-directory/
Identify bugs using Buglife's bug directory.

www.buglife.org.uk/get-involved/children-and-schools/
The children and schools' section of the Buglife website has activities and ideas
for how to get involved and save the small things that run our planet.

www.buglife.org.uk/get-involved/gardening-for-bugs/planting-for-bugs-2/
Find out which plants help insects the most. Get your whole family involved
to make your garden, or front step, a more wildlife-friendly, area.

NATIONAL INSECT WEEK

www.nationalinsectweek.co.uk/
Look out for the next National Insect Week, run by the Royal Entomological Society.

WILDLIFE TRUSTS

www.wildlifetrusts.org/wildlife-explorer/invertebrates
Explore the invertebrates' section of the Wildlife Trust website.
Go to your local wildlife trust reserve to get up close to fascinating bugs.

NATIONAL TRUST

www.nationaltrust.org.uk/features/no-31-make-friends-with-a-bug
Make friends with a bug, number 31 of its '50 things to do before
you're 11 ³/₄', and have fun exploring nature with the other 49 suggestions.

INDEX

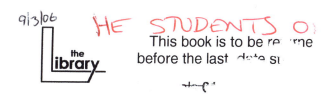